Susan Steggall's illustrations are intricate collages created from many different kinds of manufactured and handmade papers. Her books for Frances Lincoln include *On the Road, The Life of a Car, Busy Boats, Red Car, Red Bus, The Diggers are Coming!* and *Following the Tractor.* Susan lives with her family in the New Forest, Hampshire. Find out more about Susan Steggall's books at www.susansteggall.co.uk

For Peter

JANETTA OTTER-BARRY BOOKS

With thanks to Sally and Andy Barr at East Lenham Farm and to Peter Lamb in Broadchalke.

Text and illustrations © Susan Steggall 2014

First published in Great Britain and the USA in 2014 by
Frances Lincoln Children's Books
74-77 White Lion Street
London, N1 9PF

First paperback edition published in Great Britain in 2015

A CIP catalogue record for this book is available from the British Library.

ISBN: 978-1-84780-657-4

Printed in China

1 3 5 7 9 8 6 4 2

Following the Tractor

Susan Steggall

Frances Lincoln
Children's Books

The winter soil is sleeping,
when the tractor comes along,
pulling its plough through
the cold, hard ground.

And the birds fly down,
to see what can be found,
by following the tractor
around and around.

Then the tractor brings a seed drill,
to sow the soil with seeds,

and the birds fly down,
to see what can be found.

And the tractor brings a spreader,
to fertilise the fields.

And the rain comes down, down and down.
The farmer's old car gets stuck in the mud.

And still the rain comes down.

But then, the sun comes out,
and the seeds come up.

And they grow, **and they grow, and they grow.**

Until the summer soil is scorching
when the harvester comes,
rattling its reels across the hot, hard ground.

And the birds fly down,
to see what can be found,
by following the harvester around and around.

Then a big truck comes,
to carry the grain to the mill,

the tractor brings a baler,
to bale up the straw on the hill,

and the tractor brings a trailer,

to carry the straw to the farm.

But when the winter brings a chill,

the tractor's safe inside the barn.

So, the tractor, it is sleeping
when the farmer comes along,
lugging his load across the cold, hard ground.

And the cows come down,
to see what can be found,
by following the farmer around and around.

More **Busy Wheels** books by Susan Steggall from
Frances Lincoln Children's Books

Busy Boats
"Perfect for sharing with a group of children at story time or with a
single child at bedtime." – *Carousel*

On the Road
"The bold collage images of diggers, fire engines, cyclists whizzing by and the little
Mini into which the family has piled, are hugely attractive . . ." – *The Guardian*

The Diggers are coming!
"Susan Steggall's super-vivid collage illustrations of bulldozers, trucks and cranes leap
from the pages of . . . her amazing account of what happens in one year on an
urban building site." – *The Independent on Sunday*

The Life of a Car
"A simply splendid introduction to the life of a car. The pictures are bursting
with colour and will encourage children to talk about their
own experiences." – *Books for Keeps*

Red Car, Red Bus
"A joy of a book for its simplicity and vigour . . . Wonderful." – *Love Reading*

Frances Lincoln titles are available from all good bookshops.
You can also buy books and find out more about your favourite titles,
authors and illustrators on our website: www.franceslincoln.com